ULTIMATE FANTASY ART

Heroes of History and Myth

PowerKiDS press

JUAN CALLE AND WILLIAM POTTER

Published in 2020 by **The Rosen Publishing Group, Inc.**
29 East 21st Street, New York, NY 10010

Cataloging-in-Publication Data

Names: Calle, Juan. | Potter, William.
Title: Heroes of history and myth / Juan Calle and William Potter.
Description: New York : PowerKids Press, 2020. | Series: Ultimate fantasy art | Includes glossary
and index.
Identifiers: ISBN 9781725303225 (pbk.) | ISBN 9781725303249 (library bound) |
ISBN 9781725303232 (6pack)
Subjects: LCSH: | Fantasy in art--Juvenile literature. | Drawing--Technique--Juvenile literature.
Classification: LCC NC825.F25 C355 2020 | DDC 741.2--dc23

Manufactured in the United States of America

CPSIA Compliance Information: Batch CSPK19: For Further Information contact Rosen Publishing,
New York, New York at 1-800-237-9932.

CONTENTS

FANTASY COMES TO LIFE!

Welcome to the world of fantasy! From pirate captains to fairy queens, there are many mythical heroes to create in this book.

All you need to get started is a pencil and paper, but here are a few more tools you can use to add some extra magic.

Pencils come in various hardnesses—H for hard, B for soft. A 2H pencil is good for making light marks that don't smudge, and 2B for adding softer finishes for feathers, fur, and smoke. Try different hardnesses to find those you're most comfortable with. You'll also need a sharpener and eraser.

Collect pictures to inspire you. Models and figurines are also useful as reference for drawing your own fantasy folk.

Any paper will do for drawing on, especially for early sketches and planning. If you use water-based paints, you may want to use a thicker paper that absorbs the paint without it spreading—or bleeding—across the surface.

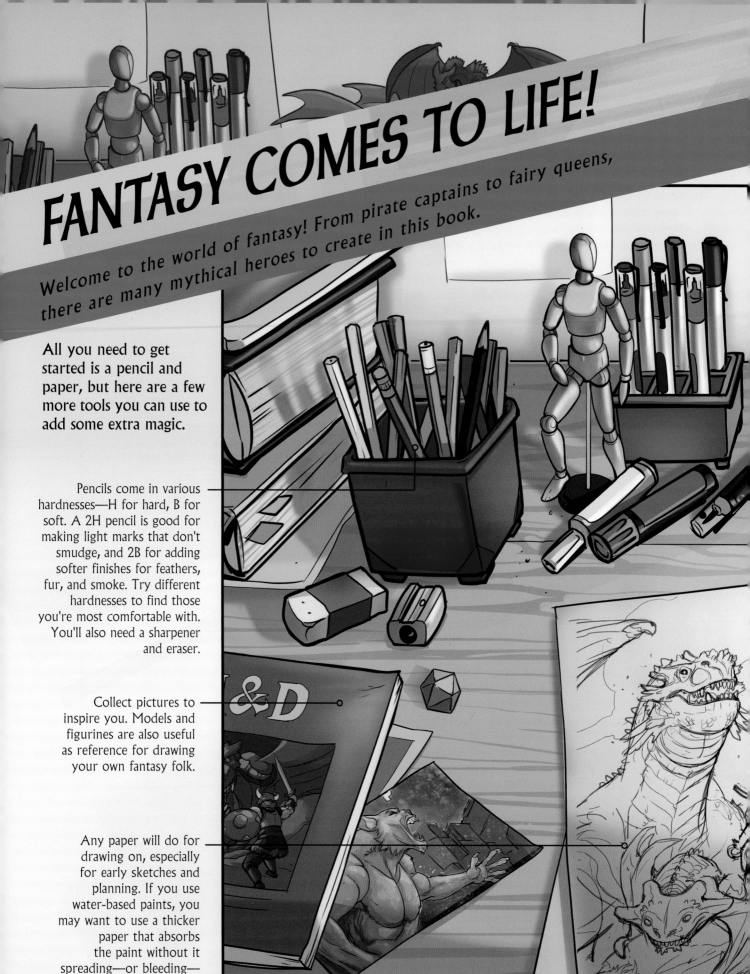

You can use a waterproof ink pen to go over your pencil lines before painting. Alternatively, use a nib pen or a fine brush dipped in ink. Using a brush and ink requires some patience and a steady hand but can produce impressive results.

For the finished picture use a range of brushes with water-based or acrylic paints, plus a tray or plate to mix different shades.

While many fantasy lands are full of forests, craggy mountains, and crumbling ruins, you may still need to use a ruler as a guide for straight weapons, buildings, mechanical devices, and planning the perspective of an action scene.

PERSPECTIVE AND PALETTES

A little knowledge of 3-D shapes and perspective goes a long way in helping the most incredible scene look real.

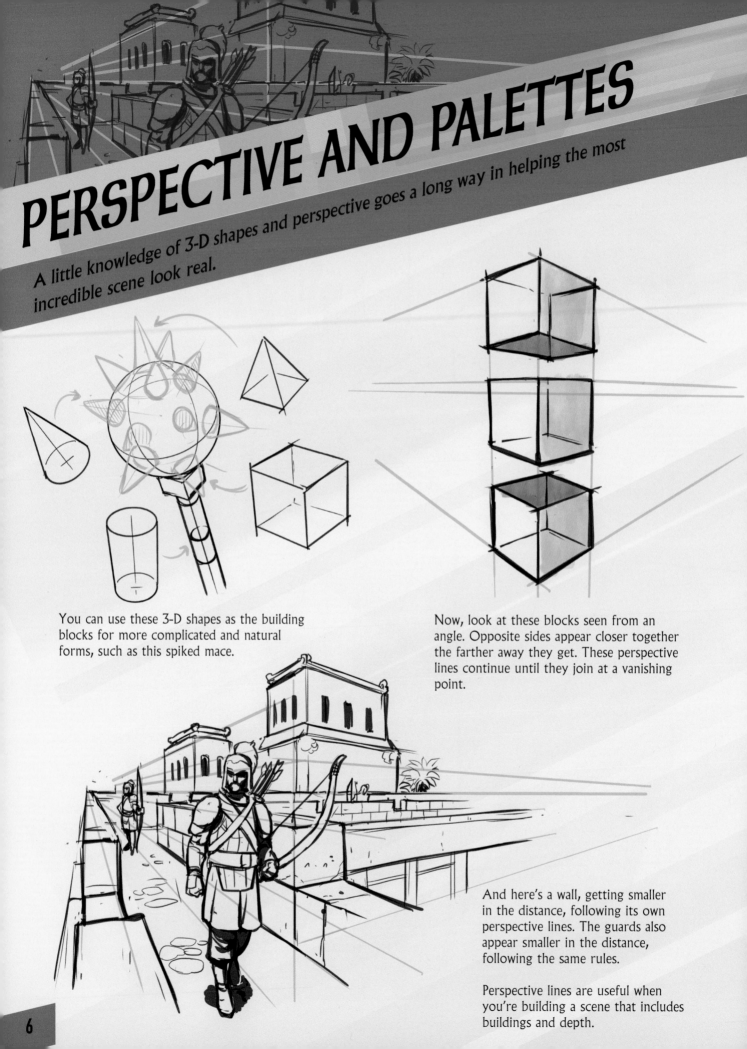

You can use these 3-D shapes as the building blocks for more complicated and natural forms, such as this spiked mace.

Now, look at these blocks seen from an angle. Opposite sides appear closer together the farther away they get. These perspective lines continue until they join at a vanishing point.

And here's a wall, getting smaller in the distance, following its own perspective lines. The guards also appear smaller in the distance, following the same rules.

Perspective lines are useful when you're building a scene that includes buildings and depth.

Reds suggest blood, fire, and passion. Use these to raise the temperature of your fantasy scenes.

Browns and greens are calming, reminding you of nature. Many adventures involve quests across countrysides. Create drama by beginning a journey in a relaxing green environment and transitioning to a more threatening domain of red and black.

Blues are cooler. They suggest frosty, unfeeling, ghostly moods.

OUT OF TIME

History is rich with tales of knights, samurai, and pirates, while myths tell of gods and humans on quests to face monsters. Here is a handful of legendary figures you could add to your tales.

PIRATE CAPTAIN

How do you keep a rowdy pirate crew under control? By being the toughest and most dangerous pirate aboard the ship! Quick with a cutlass or pistol, this pirate captain demands utmost loyalty, and rewards her crew well. Years at sea raiding cargo ships, and fighting navies and rivals, have bred a captain as wild as the seas she sails.

PIRATE STYLE

Life at sea is not for the fainthearted. The captain is dressed in tough leathers battered by bitter storms. Leather belts and straps hold pistols and gunpowder. A scarf is tied around her braided, flame-red hair. Her teeth are gritted with determination.

VIKING RAIDER

The ancient past is filled with tales of armies on the battlefield. You could recruit Spartans, Assyrians, or Celts for your sagas. Or how about a Viking raider? Like his god, Thor, he wields a hammer and threatens to bring a thunderous storm to the shores of distant lands. He is a "berserker," the most feared Viking raider, a warrior who works himself into a furious rage before battle.

VIKING STYLE

The Viking appears not to feel the cold. He wears a simple leather kilt but his chest and legs are bare. When the bitter north winds blow, he wraps himself in a cloak cut from the skin of a white bear he killed himself. The fur adds to his animal-like appearance. His eyes are wide open from his berserker rage, and his mouth roars a battle cry.

MONKEY GOD

Fantasy characters do not all have to resemble humans. The monkey god of Eastern legend is half-human, half-ape in form, has huge strength, the ability to change his size at will, and can leap vast distances. He would make a formidable addition to your fables, as a fighter or sage. While able to defend himself in battle, this hero also possesses great wisdom.

MONKEY GOD STYLE

The monkey god can stand up straight like a human but has the facial features, hands, feet, and tail of a monkey. His clothes are made from the finest gilded fabrics. His head and arm ornaments glitter with gold and gems. In his hand, he carries a decorated mace as a sign of his power more than as a weapon.

SWORDSWOMAN

Don't be deceived by looks. A beauty could be a beast, or a princess a soldier. This self-taught sword fighter was invited to the palace by the king to instruct his troops. Her skill with a sword is legendary. Her deft, elegant moves put stronger opponents to shame. She appears at peace during combat, expending the minimum of effort with devastating results.

SWORDSWOMAN STYLE

This swordswoman is dressed in flowing silk robes, but she exudes an inner strength. Her face shows little emotion as she is focused on battle, striking a martial-arts pose, and holding her long sword as an extension of her body. She is a true living weapon.

NOBLE SAMURAI

The samurai, or bushi, were a warrior class that ruled Japan for centuries. While adept with bows, spears, and guns, they were most known for their sword skills.

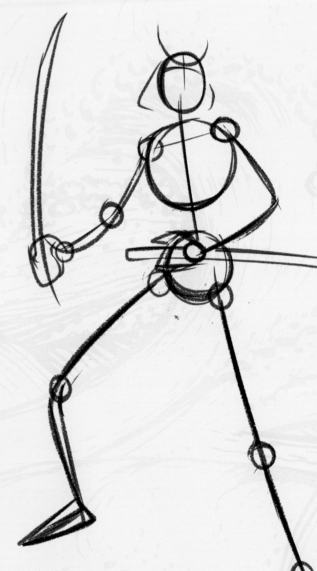

1. STICK FIGURE
Using light pencil marks, draw a simple stick figure showing your samurai's pose, with lines for his sword and sheath. He has just taken out his sword, and raises it to show he is ready for battle.

2. JOINTED FIGURE
Now, use circles to indicate the position of the samurai's joints. The left leg is held straight, while the right leg is bent at the knee.

4. FINISHED PENCILS

Now tighten your pencils. The triangular helmet includes a wide neck guard and horns. The face mask is designed to look like a fierce warrior.

3. ANATOMY

Sketch the outline of the helmeted figure, with rectangular shapes for his protective clothing. His heavy outfit is made of strips of iron and leather, bound together in rows.

5. PALETTE

When you are happy with your drawing, choose the range of shades you want to use on the figure. This samurai's tough clothing is painted with blues linked with red ribbons of silk over dark underclothes.

TOP TIP

Samurai helmets, or kabuto, were designed to protect the head and neck. Crests could represent family, animals, or mythical beings. Here are some variations you can use or adapt for your own Japanese warrior.

6. FINAL ART
The finished painting adds highlights to the tough strips that form the protective outerwear. His sword has dark and light curved streaks added to it. Very little of the face is seen beneath the intimidating mask.

FAIRY QUEEN

The fairy queen is a woodland spirit who protects the animals that live in her realm. She wears many disguises, but appears to the fortunate few as a winged maiden.

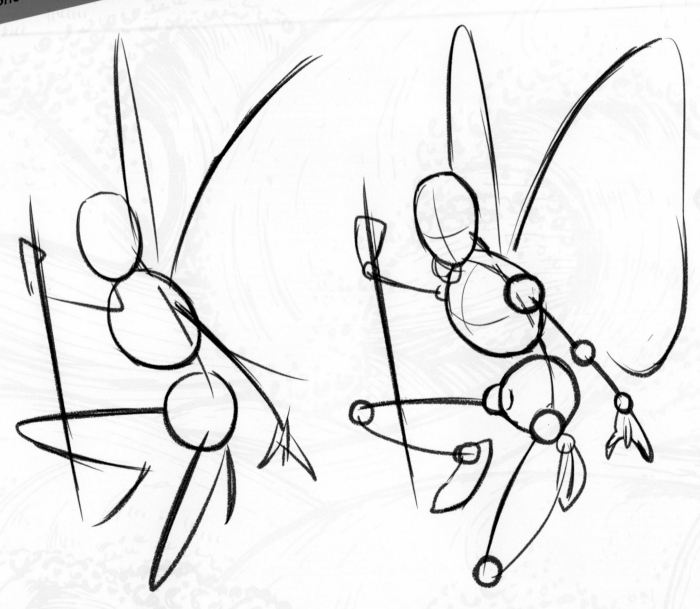

1. STICK FIGURE
Using light pencil marks, draw a simple stick figure showing your fairy queen's crouching pose, and the outline of her wings and sword.

2. JOINTED FIGURE
Use a cross to indicate the front of her face and eyeline. Use circles to mark the position of her arms and leg joints.

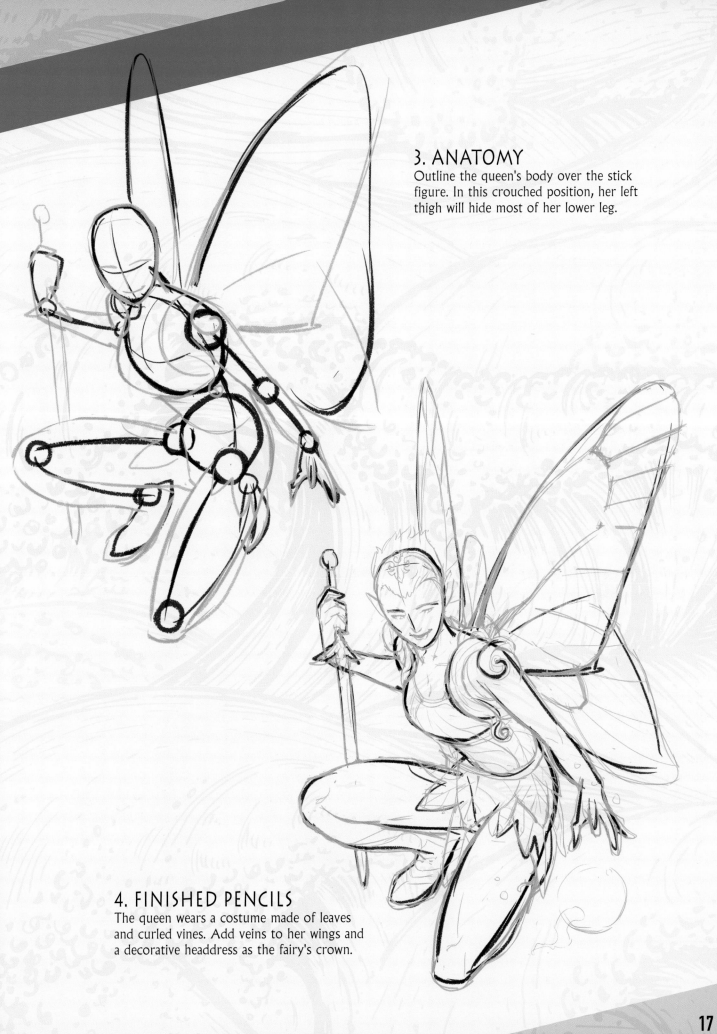

3. ANATOMY
Outline the queen's body over the stick figure. In this crouched position, her left thigh will hide most of her lower leg.

4. FINISHED PENCILS
The queen wears a costume made of leaves and curled vines. Add veins to her wings and a decorative headdress as the fairy's crown.

TOP TIP

This fairy queen's wings are based on those of a butterfly. Like a church's stained-glass windows, they are built from a frame of black outlines, each filled with one shade. Close up, each shape contains tiny scales. Paler shades are semitransparent.

5. PALETTE

The fairy queen belongs to the forest, so use leafy greens for her dress. In contrast, use vibrant blues and pinks for her wings.

6. FINAL ART

In the finished painting, the fairy queen is lit by the magical blue spirit she conjures in her hand. The wings are painted in pastel shades and partly transparent. Her hair is an ageless, lighter shade of purple.

LONE KNIGHT

Knights of old times wore heavy iron or steel plating to protect them from arrow and sword attacks, or during jousting events. Here's how to dress a knight ready for war.

CHAIN MAIL

Where the body was not covered by solid metal, or where the knight needed more movement at his elbows and waist, he would wear chain mail, woven from rows of fine metal rings. Chain mail offered less protection against arrows or sword thrusts.

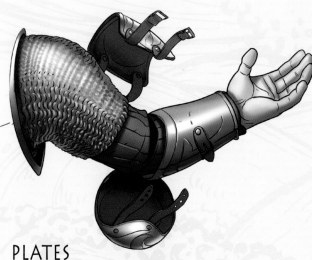

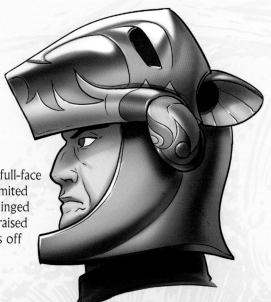

PLATES

A medieval knight was protected by a series of metal plates, held together by rivets and straps. The plates divided at the joints to allow movement. Below the plates, the knight wore padded garments.

HELMET

This intimidating, full-face helmet provides limited vision, but has a hinged visor that can be raised when the knight is off the battlefield.

BATTLE READY

Covered in so much plating, the identity of the knight remains a mystery. The fine etching on his helmet, shoulder, and chest plates suggest he is wealthy or a high-ranking knight. Only the symbol on his shield offers a clue to the knight's origin.

FANTASY FORTRESS

Imposing and almost impregnable, a fortress is a sign of wealth and power. Follow the steps to create your own stronghold for a noble king, ready for an attack by an enemy army.

2. PERSPECTIVE

Use a ruler to draw perspective lines to show the angle of the fortress walls and towers. Towers have been built on top of towers as different kings have tried to improve fortifications.

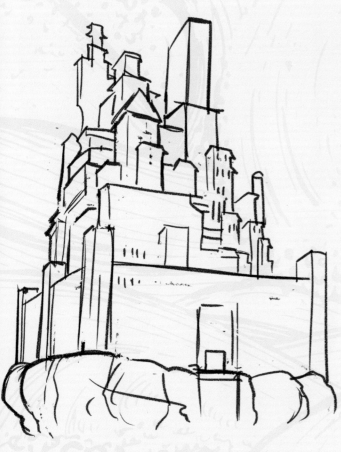

1. BUILDING PLAN

This rough sketch shows the fortress as seen from below. The castle is built on a high cliff, and from this angle, it looks impossible to break into.

3. PALETTE

The fortress is built from local stone, a reddish brick. Some high towers have bluish tiles on the roof.

4. FULLY CONSTRUCTED

In the finished image, the highest towers disappear in storm clouds. This helps suggest the fortress is immensely tall, and adds a sense of menace to the scene. Is the castle doomed or is it ruled by some sinister power?

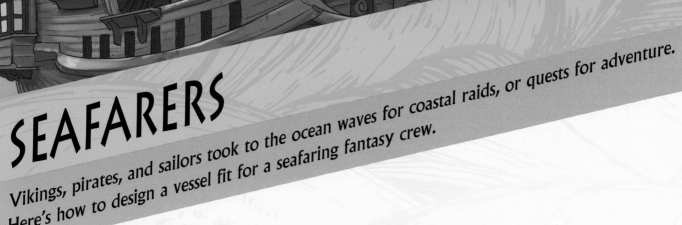

SEAFARERS

Vikings, pirates, and sailors took to the ocean waves for coastal raids, or quests for adventure. Here's how to design a vessel fit for a seafaring fantasy crew.

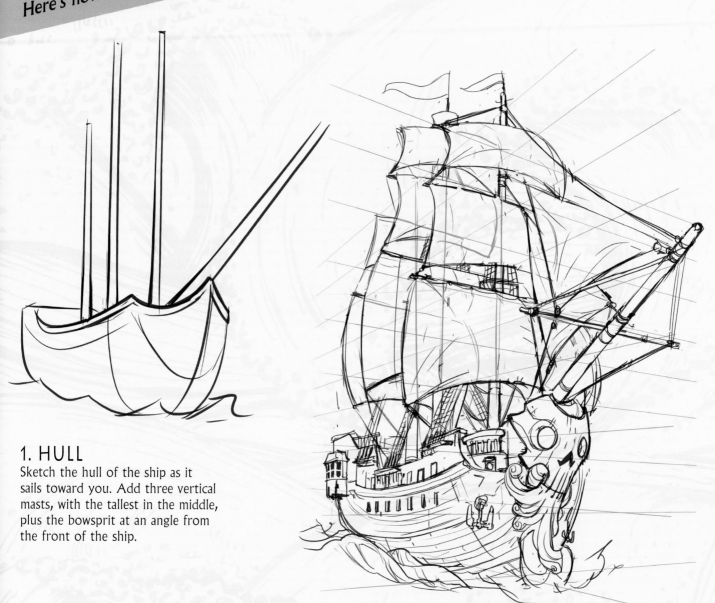

1. HULL

Sketch the hull of the ship as it sails toward you. Add three vertical masts, with the tallest in the middle, plus the bowsprit at an angle from the front of the ship.

2. SAILS

Now draw the sails hanging from the wooden yardarms on each vertical mast. Use perspective lines to help with the correct angles. This pirate ship has a menacing, skull-like figurehead on the bow.

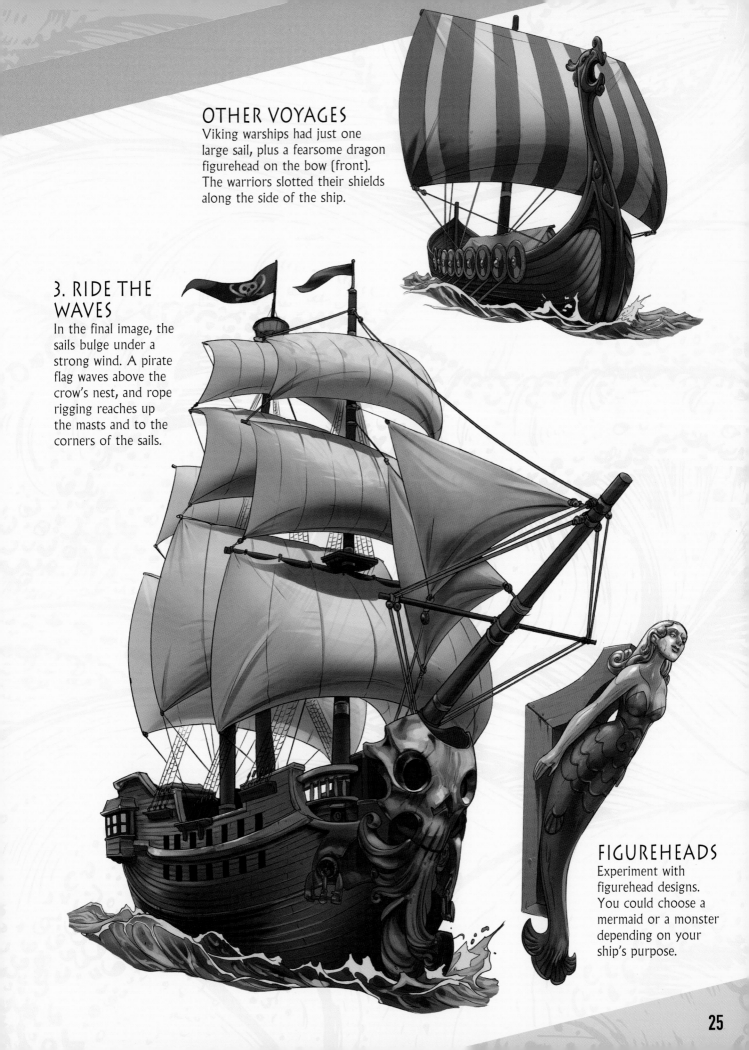

OTHER VOYAGES

Viking warships had just one large sail, plus a fearsome dragon figurehead on the bow (front). The warriors slotted their shields along the side of the ship.

3. RIDE THE WAVES

In the final image, the sails bulge under a strong wind. A pirate flag waves above the crow's nest, and rope rigging reaches up the masts and to the corners of the sails.

FIGUREHEADS

Experiment with figurehead designs. You could choose a mermaid or a monster depending on your ship's purpose.

UNDER SIEGE

A coastal town is under attack by a creature from the deep. A pirate crew has been caught in the conflict. Follow the steps to create a dramatic scene of monsters and mariners.

1. This rough plan of the scene has pirates aboard the ship in the foreground, right, directing their harpoons toward a massive squid monster that is tearing down the town.

2. Perpective lines show how the scene is viewed from a dramatic angle. All the action is directed toward the monster.

3. In these tighter pencils, shading has been added. This helps bring order to the frenzied fight. Crashing waves toss smaller boats into the air. One large tentacle in the foreground threatens to squeeze the ship and crew.

4. The monster is painted in blood red, contrasting with the turquoise of the seawater and sky. The frothing foam on the waves is streaked and splashed with white.

UNDER SIEGE CONTINUED

The finished scene is a chaotic clash of writhing red tentacles, wreckage, and raging waters.

GLOSSARY

3-D Three-dimensional, which means having length, breadth, and depth.

anatomy The human body.

Assyrians People from an ancient civilization in what is now northern Iraq and southeastern Turkey.

bowsprit A pole running from the front of a ship.

Celts A group of people who lived in ancient Britain and parts of Western Europe.

crow's nest A lookout platform at the top of a ship's mast.

cutlass A short, curved sword.

fable A short story intended to teach a moral lesson.

figurehead A carved bust or full figure placed on the front of a ship.

highlight The white area that helps to make a drawing look solid and draw attention to its shape.

mace A heavy club used as a weapon.

mariners People who navigate a ship.

palette The range of shades chosen by an artist.

perspective The representation on a flat surface of a three-dimensional image as seen by the eye, to give the illusion of distance and depth.

rigging Ropes attached to a ship's sails.

sagas Stories about heroes and legendary events in the ancient literature of Iceland.

sage A person of great wisdom.

Spartans People from Sparta, an ancient Greek city-state.

Thor The Viking god of thunder, weather, and crops.

vanishing point The point at which parallel lines seem to meet in the distance.

visor The front piece of a helmet.

yardarms The ends of long, horizontal beams attached to the mast of a ship, used for spreading the sails.

FURTHER INFORMATION

Books

Alexander, Rob, and Finlay Cowan and Kevin Walker. *The Compendium of Fantasy Art Techniques*. Hauppauge, NY: Barron's, 2014.

Blando, Jared. *How to Draw Fantasy Art and RPG Maps*. Cincinnati, OH: Impact Books, 2015.

Cook, Trevor, and Lisa Miles. *Drawing Fantasy Figures.* New York, NY: Gareth Stevens Publishing, 2011.

Websites

Art for Kids Hub

www.artforkidshub.com/how-to-draw

This website has instructions for drawing all sorts of things.

How to Draw Castles in 5 Steps

lifestyle.howstuffworks.com/crafts/drawing/how-to-draw-castles.htm

Follow the instructions on this page to draw a magnificent castle!

Publisher's note to educators and parents: Our editors have carefully reviewed these websites to ensure that they are suitable for students. Many websites change frequently, however, and we cannot guarantee that a site's future contents will continue to meet our high standards of quality and educational value. Be advised that students should be closely supervised whenever they access the Internet.

INDEX

A
anatomy 13, 17
armor 20–21
Assyrians 9

B
battles 9, 10, 12, 20, 26–29
brushes 5

C
captains 8
Celts 9
China 11
clothes 8, 9, 10, 11, 14–15,
    18–19, 20–21
colors 7, 14–15, 18–19,
    23, 27–29

F
fairies 16–19
figureheads 25
fortresses 22–23

G
gods 9, 10

H
helmets 12–15, 20–21

J
Japan 12–15

K
kings 11, 22
knights 8, 20–21

M
monkey god 10
monsters 26–29

P
painting 4, 5, 15, 19
palettes 7, 14–15, 18–19,
    23, 27–29
paper, pens, and pencils 4–5
perspective 5, 6, 22, 24, 26
pirates 8, 24, 26–29

Q
queens 16–19

S
Samurai 12–15
ships 8, 24–25, 26–29
Spartans 9

V
vanishing point 6
Vikings 9, 24, 25

W
warriors 9, 12–15
weapons 8, 9, 10, 11, 12
    bows 12
    cutlass 8
    guns 12
    hammer 9
    mace 6
    pistol 8
    spears 12
    swords 8, 11, 12–15
wings 16–19